tide pool of words

*prose and poetry from a
beach chair storyteller*

Robert A. Cozzi

TIDE POOL OF WORDS

Beach Umbrella Publishing
130 Beachfield Drive
Rehoboth Beach, Delaware, USA 19971

Printed in the United States of America

First Edition – 2013

The publisher is not responsible for websites (or their content)
that are not owned by the publisher.

ISBN-13: 978-1490966328
ISBN-10: 1490966323

Cataloging-in-publication data is on file with the Library of
Congress.

I would like to dedicate
this book of work:

To Gerard Yatcilla for encouraging
me to write something new every week

To Bobby Croker for writing the
music that inspired so many of the pieces in
this book

To Mom, Dad, and Annmarie *with
love...*

Foreword

I first met Robby in 1992 when we worked for the same hotel and even though we were in very different life places, we quickly became friends. I was in school for graphic design at the time and he always would ask to see my drawings and offer words of encouragement. The foundation of that relationship was built on trust and mutual admiration that withstood over 18 years of no communication.

When we reconnected through social media a couple of years ago, that relationship was as strong as ever, and we were delighted to learn that we were both still working creatively. He was still writing and I was composing music, and we were both still very inspired by the ocean. We told each other stories about the beach and how often that inspiration makes it into our work. I shared with him my love of Rehoboth Beach, Delaware, often sending pictures from my favorite spots.

Meanwhile, he was finding inspiration for his words through my pictures and music. He started to send me pieces he had written based on my work which further inspired me and then that grew into every note, every passage, and every phrase becoming a musical interpretation of both his words and my pictures. His practice of posting new words every Sunday morning became my ritual and I still check for his new words every Sunday before even rolling out of bed.

Robby's talent really shines through in his ability to both transport you through a memory and to evoke specific emotions. When I read his words I KNOW the people he writes about, I know WHERE he is, and I FEEL what he is feeling because his empathy allows him to express things that we ALL feel. The memories might be his but the feelings are universal.

We've all lost loved ones, we've all been in love, we've all been hurt, and we've all felt joy. He is able to sum up those intense, complex emotions with just a few carefully selected words, and that is how he has been able to inspire me. The bond two artists share through mutual inspiration is very special, and I'm so honored and grateful that I share that with him. I hope Robby is able to inspire all of his readers as much as he does me!

Bobby Croker
http://soundtcloud.com/bobby-croker

Words of praise for
Robert A. Cozzi

"I can only describe Robby as a writing artist; he's like a painter of words.
Just like a wonderful painting can touch the deepest parts of you, so Robby reaches into you
with a canvas of delicately described details and descriptive imagery.
I often find myself drifting off into thoughts of things long forgotten when I read Robby's words, he has a way of sparking trains of thought and drawing things out of you that have long
been packaged up and put into storage.
I like that, his words have meditative qualities,
I always come away feeling that all is good in the world."
Ian Tompkins, *Musician*, Nottingham, England

"Both the prose and poetry of Mr. Cozzi are rich and lyrical, almost painterly in their descriptiveness. Reading his work, one is gently taken away to different places and emotions, deposited for those moments into scenes that enrich the reader with their authenticity and feeling."
Karin Tirell-Hoffmann, Bel Air, MD

"When I read something Robby has written it is like an expansion of horizons only to be whisked away into a fairy tale land of serendipity. Robby writes from the very depths of his soul and I cherish the memory of when we met. Through writing is how we met and I shall never forget that day"
Morgan Ansons, *Author*, *Poet*, Philadelphia, PA

OCEAN DREAM

Whenever I sleep at the shore
I dream in aquamarine shades
With soft autumn highlights
In an ocean so blue

Salty air whispers inside the wind
As the slow rush of waves
Wash away the stresses of the day

I awake
To the sounds of children laughing
and splashing

In the golden sun....

AMONGST THE RAIN

The clouds are shedding tears
again
The wind is whistling a bold
refrain
Mist dances on the rooftops with
the tar
Red bricks are soaking rain
instead of light

Cold fingers trace the raindrops on
the window
Mosaics of umbrellas line the
street
Soft music gently sweeps across
the porch
And tired, hungry feelings go to
sleep

There's wisdom in accepting
sudden changes
And beauty in adapting to their
pace
There's strength in letting go of
angry questions
So hope may grace another sunny
day

Before... and... After

He floated for hours

In the oceans of your eyes

Tasted the clouds

From your lips

Wondering...

Where else would

Your love take him?

He craved that journey ...

But now...

He shields himself

Under the ruse of fear

That the drops of rain

Will soak into his soul

And find that

He too

Is as elusive as a raindrop

SIDE BY SIDE

The cool ocean breeze
Saunters onto the back deck
Where we sit together side by side
Enjoying our fresh tomato sandwiches
After a pristine day at the beach

Here... We are set apart
From the rest of the house
With one lone lamp burning
That lights your eyes
With mischievous teasing
That makes my face turn red

I snuggle close
Fitting perfectly into the recesses of
you
Slipping between the grooves
We are sleek perfection
We are...
One....

BUOYANCY

Screen door dreams
Mesh and wet
Sand and salt
An undivided ocean

The volume of a smile
As open as that door
No shadows blow
In the trail of a breeze

Upon waves and words
We dine on possibilities
Like gulls fishing
From sunlit piers

The horizon swells
Within the circle of our reach
Waist bound and anchored
But infinite as faith
And a sea of belief

EMPTY BEACH

There is almost no wind
Waves caress the empty beach

Seagulls circle above looking for
breakfast
In the east the sun begins its
assent

As the day commences in
thundering silence
I miss you in this, another place
we have never shared

Robert A. Cozzi

GONE

Gone…
The warmth
Of shared connections
And the evening revelry
Of touching souls

Gone…
Orchestral overtures
The heart's wand
Conducting our symphony

Gone…
The intimate
Pure scent
Of love…

WORKING IN
THE BACKYARD

Here...

*From his chair on the back
porch...*

He stares up at the birds

Flying to the sun

*Signaling the transition... from
today... to tomorrow...*

RAINBOW COLORED NIGHTS IN REHOBOTH

Night walks in

Confronted by time's revelations

*Windows glare from rainbow
colored lights*

Their reflections reveal much

Deep between the lines they travel

And tell what is truly needed

For life

And its magical spell

While pending sleep

Finally calls out my name

THE JERSEY SHORE WILL RISE AGAIN

The crystal blue ocean tide is reticent to part

While you are in mid-sentence

On your writing tablet

And the day slows

Knowing you're not ready to leave

As you dig your feet

Deep

Into the cold sand

Rooting

Bruce plays on your iPod

"Land of Hope and Dreams"

You stop writing

And close your eyes softly

To listen

His words resonate

And

The shore

Once battered and bruised

All at once

Becomes beautiful

And whole again…

A HUNDRED THOUSAND PIECES OF SEA GLASS

I can't talk right now
My mind is full
With indistinct hope
And fear
And disappointment
The weight of the world spread out
Like a blanket on the beach
Sun baked
My words have dissipated
Like water vapor in the sky
Floating miniscule
Beyond the range of sight

But I feel them
And I think maybe something inside me
Would like to break the rules
Smash the globe that holds the status quo
And walk through a hundred thousand
Pieces of glass
To feel
Invigorated

But in the meantime
The pressure builds
As I collect the world
Like the dark clouds
That form slowly above the ocean
Waiting for the right moment
To speak

Robert A. Cozzi

WHISPERING TO THE SEA

Sometimes the blustery wind sings
Quietly
Behind the patter of eager raindrops
On the roof and windows
Of this old back porch

As I listen
Pictures of you
Spiral before my eyes
Each one gently bouncing off the other
In a kaleidoscope of presaging memories

Sometimes
I whisper
"I love you too"
To your imaginary shadow
Dancing on my wall

JERSEY STRONG

Even the birds are shivering

Orange and red leaves are now brown

Savagely thrown to the ground by Sandy

Inside, we huddle in layers of clothes and blankets

Just trying to get through the night

While our minds race, refusing to stop

I finally heard from the last loved one

He is safe

And that gives me some temporary peace of mind

Winter nights are near

I worry about the ones who lost the most

*And empty my closet of the warm clothes I
no longer wear*

The shelter near my house needs these

*The images on the news are almost too much
to take*

*It's a call to action for those of us already
back on our feet*

To reach back and pull someone else up

*Jon Bon Jovi and The Boss have already
gotten the ball rolling*

*And so has my cousin Mark, who has been
cooking and serving meals to his fellow
residents of Jersey City*

This is my first night with power

But I am as restless as ever

And at my kitchen sink, washing the dishes

On my iPod

The old Pat Benatar song, "We Belong"
plays

And these lines that I have heard a million
times before

Stop me in my tracks

"Whatever we deny or embrace… for worse
or for better…we belong… together."

Just beyond the flickering candle on the
windowsill

I see a horizon bright

Adorning this chilly November morning

A new sky is here, New Jersey

And you are not in this alone…

Robert A. Cozzi

THE CAPE

Slipping and sliding

Down memory lane

Stealing waves

From the chilly ocean waters of The Cape

Hitting tennis balls with the local boys

*The ever present Yankees/Red Sox debate
raging*

Batman kite flying high above the dunes

Giving myself

To the hands of time

Rapidly rewinding

I'm dreaming summer

GETTING THROUGH TO THE OTHER SIDE

Left and right steps mar the floor
Echoing the steady clack of thoughts
dripping through my consciousness
I can hear the sound of broken promises
shattering in the air around me
I remember believing them once
Promises had slid so easily from his lips
Cancer growing inside each one

I tried to cling to their remnants
But the shards tore me open

Left to right
The clacking faded to memory
The days crept by
Until they were nothing more than
shadows
That waned on the hard wood floor
In the room around me

Robert A. Cozzi

DIAGNOSIS LOVE

There is a small glass table
Nestled in a garden
And on a soft summer's night
Two friends sit closely together
Under the night sky

The conversation flows
Though they often stop to think
The topics they cover range far
and wide
And the glasses of ginger beer
Poured hours ago
Sit there empty

The night is getting cooler
But the friends stay
close and warm

The crescent moon looks down at
them calmly
And in perfect time
Spins a magical spotlight below
Just as he leans across for a kiss

Making the friendship
In an instant
Into something much more

REWINDING MOMENTS

*Rewinding moments are passing
me by*

In some of them I hear laughter

And in others I see tears

*They appear softer each time I
think of you*

And louder as I start to miss you

The day folds into night

And the moon smiles down

*Delicately inviting me to the
evening's slumber*

As the morning crawls in

Another sunrise blankets the sky

Inching me closer

To the sun that rises in my heart

THE MOURNFUL SOUND OF THE 11:20 TRAIN

I see a star filled sky
The night air is musky and cool
The mournful sound of the
11:20 train
Is heard rolling down its tracks

Pair of eyes glint in the darkness
Gazing at the stars
And wishing that someone
Perhaps someone like me
Is looking at them too

WILD HEARTS

Your music touches my forehead
Kissing my soul
My words whisper in your ears
Touching your spirit

Silk strands of imagination
Turn words into pristine music
Bands of desire
Wrap tightly around

While silvery images of lakeside
gazebos
Shelter our wild hearts

SUMMER LOVE

I carry the images
Of our beach dream
In my pocket
So it can never fade away

I want to breathe in the salt
From the ocean's air
And taste the gliding wind
That arrives over cresting waves

I imagine you chasing me
On our way into the water
Feeling the warm sand
Sifting through our toes

Laughter spills easily
From our lips
As we splash around
In the ocean waves

The crystal blue glow in your eyes
Reminds me
That we are exactly
Where we belong…

FAIRY TALE

*From here I can almost make myself
believe his world is a fairy tale that I
am reading about in a book. The
adjectives and verbs are what make me
ache and not anything real or tangible
that I will ever get my hands on.*

*If it were true, if this were a vividly
inspiring novel, then I would be
content to curl up with my favorite
book each night and pretend he is real.*

But he is real.

*And the knowledge of that makes it
almost impossible to stop myself from
plunging into the ocean and swimming
to him.*

The ocean is my sanctuary, the solitary moment of peace in my day. Without it I could not survive my nightmare. Fantasy is a gift given only to those who have been abandoned by reality. No others have a right to it. I deserve a lifetime supply.

His dog's name is Tugger and this is their special time together. They never miss a day and no one ever comes with them. I've heard that you can tell a lot about a man by his relationship with his dog. If that is true, then this man is the stuff heroes are made of.

And if he is a hero, then just maybe he can save me.

Robert A. Cozzi

FULL MOON ON
A WARM NIGHT IN MAY

I write these words
From my back porch
Anticipating May's
Shimmering moonlight
But the clouds are blocking my view

A serenade of
Night birds and crickets
Sing along to Stevie Nicks'
"Moonlight" playing on my stereo
It's the perfect soundtrack for such an
expected luminous night

The fireflies I see
Hint of summer nights to come
Lighting our way
Though the darkness
They keep us on the right path
On evenings such as this
When the moon is hidden...

RODDY AND COZZ

Distant, faded

Like a hazy vision

Rewinding, replaying

In a steady stream

No longer a silhouette

But vivid and clear

An unexpected connection

And a mutual passion for words

Seal the friendship

Giving rise to lost dreams

Breathing life into creativity, and

*Erasing impossibilities once
believed*

Robert A. Cozzi

DAYBREAK UNFOLDING

Last night I only had pockets of sleep
Mary knows how this feels
And I wonder if she's awake too
As I step outside and take a seat on the top stair

I read once somewhere that the breeze at dawn
reveals secrets
So you should never go back to sleep!
Hmmm...I wonder if this is true

On this day
The cool morning air
Dares to secretly awaken
A gentle breeze
That tickles the crooked smile on my face

Silence is all around me
Even the birds are sleeping softly
Awaiting the first kiss of sunrise
To make their presence known

Orange juice in hand
I sit in amazement
Anxiously watching
As beauty unfolds in the sky above
And that same gentle breeze
Secretly brushes my cheek
Tickling the smile
That is still on my face...

FUZZY LINES WRITTEN
AT MIDNIGHT

Just like an old train
Making its way down a battered set of
tracks
My mind rattles at twelve midnight
There is no silence in my silence
As fuzzy lines on the pages of my
journal grow bolder

I remember the dream
Your sleepy head…cradled my arms
Moving slowly like a flower in a soft
breeze
I pull you close and kiss the top
Of your peppermint scented forehead
That is nestled comfortably on my
chest

<sigh>

MAGIC HAPPENS WHEN THE
TURTLES DANCE

I love…
When the turtles come to dance
In the lake's undisturbed September water
And the way you look at me
As we share this moment
From our spot on the pier

I love…
The tiny crinkle at your eyes
As your slow forming smile
Brightens your face

I love…
The scent of peppermint oil on your skin
And the way my eyes close
As I breathe in your fragrance

I love…
How the silvery glow of the lake
Spills into our bedroom at night
Seeping through
To illuminate our dreams

I love…
You

MOONDANCE

I stretch out my legs
On my favorite porch chair
Burrowed beneath
Aunt Bette's warm afghan
And a sky full of stars

The moon shivers above
Showering the wintery night
With a shimmering glow
Illuminating even the darkest of
hours

I just love how the moon
Trades places with the sun
Finding its home perfectly
Between sunrise and sunset

Robert A. Cozzi

LOVE COMES WHEN
WE LEAST EXPECT IT

Seamlessly
Our lives travel
Through an endless array
Of days and nights

Today
This violet and blue morning
Is so beautiful
And much like you
So unaware
Of its resplendent allure

Desirous stares
Go unnoticed
(Except... maybe... for mine!)

A new sunrise
Arrives
Behind every sunset

Be sure to
Save one
To share
With a pair of eyes
That loves
Only you...

MUSIC AND SALTY AIR
SOOTHE THE SOUL

*I know you like I know the smell of the
salty air that gusts
Above the shoreline in summer
The way the sky looks right before the
thunder booms
Even when the sun is shining brightly
And the way the rain sounds bouncing
off the roof
When I'm lying in bed*

*Today
Your music soothes my anxiety
And calms the tides of my impatience
That rush over me*

*I know one day you will press your
palms against my cheeks
And gently kiss my forehead and tell
me it was worth the wait
I know one day I will fall asleep in
your arms*

And forget that I ever knew life without
you

Or that I ever restlessly wondered if
someone
Like you really existed

I know
That never again
Will I ever
Feel
Alone

WRITING MY WAY OUT OF THE SHADOWS

Sometimes we exist on the lips of anxiety
Staring down cold, desolate walls
People whisper quietly down these hallways as they pass
Not knowing how fear runs like water
Through each one of your veins

REOCCUR

The skies rupture
Early spring air fills the porch
with freshness
The falling water feeds the plants
and trees
Cleansing them in preparation
For winter's end

Mirror on the ground
Formed by tears of joy from up
above
Gives glimpses of new creations
Wading through heart and soul
Shortly unfurling
Life
As it prepares to reoccur

FROM DARKNESS
COMES LIGHT

It was a wicked dream

I hate the nightmares when they come

*Feeling cold in the darkness of the early
morning*

I wearily make my way to the shower

Passing a smiling photo of you on the way

And

Just like your smile

The water warms me

As your essence stretches across

My heart's skyline

Eclipsing my edginess

Making me smile

While the memories of you

Return

And once again

Come alive

Robert A. Cozzi

MATT'S MUSIC

His Emotions
Run like wet paint on the canvas
And spill over from page to page
Beautiful graffiti made from the heart
For all to see
And as he pens a new song
He gives it all
Takes very little
Expects even less
Passing on his wisdom
To help us through

Selfless and generous to a fault
He tells the tale of a broken love affair
That came and went
Traced with complexities
Like sand castles at high tide
It washed away, ever so slowly
But the memories remain

He sits at his beloved korg
His faithful companion in times of strife
As he tries to fit all the pieces
Of his heart, his song
Back together

Like torn pages, glued together
He begins again

LIFE GOES ON

Month of dreams
Promises unspoken
Kisses nestled
In the magic of starry nights

Whispers of fantasies
Drained from this pen
Capture moments
From a heart of sighs…

DANCING THROUGH TIDE POOLS

*He closed his eyes and listened to
the chanting of the rain.*

*Watching the ceaseless pitter-
patter of the rain broke the
tranquility in the room.*

*Clouds were trying to catch the
glow of the sun that was busy
creating zigzag patterns on the
windowpanes.*

*He pulled out his black umbrella
and stepped out into the rain,
which was falling in sheets and
turning the ground into a soup of
mud and leaves.*

He swiftly crossed the broken pavement, admiring the raw obsession of the torrential rains at their peak.

Jumping over puddles and looking back at his printed footsteps, he found his heart was as light as a quill.

Robert A. Cozzi

ENCOUNTER WITH
A NEW DAY

Sunlight beckons
The beginning of a new day
Yesterday is gone
A new start lies before you

All of the tears
All of the lies
All of the pain
All of the addictions
All of the guilt
Belong to yesterday

Today you are embarking on a new
adventure

Run into the light

Let it hug you

Let it love you

Let it shower you

With arms outstretched

Eagerly embrace the new day

And the new you

Your life begins now...

FAREWELL TO A LOVER

The breeze gently sways around your hair

And your deep set eyes begin to tear from
the wind

We stand there in awkward silence

Both lost in the train of our thoughts

Each of us had parallel dreams that lived
side by side

But they never got the chance to merge

I look up at the clock that says 5:30

The moment to part is coming closer

In ten minutes you will be on that
northbound train

Tide Pool of Words

People are rushing all around us and past
us…with their luggage in hand

Their boarding passes and their indicated
destinations

And still we stand there…frozen

I give you a hurried hug and turn around
slowly

Detaching myself from your eyes

Looking over my shoulder

That faraway gaze of yours
Breaks me

Without words, we say goodbye

A PERFECT SUMMER AFTERNOON

Lying next to you
Each of us engrossed in a book
I lean over
And tell you to close your eyes

As I lay my book down on your
stomach
I trace your mouth gently with my
fingertips
Your breathing quickens
And I smile at your reaction
As my kisses leave a trail of dew
upon you…

STONES IN THE WATER

The distance between
Love and here

Seemed natural at first
A sudden shifting of energies.

What was the worst
That could possibly happen?

A forlorn propensity
to need what couldn't be said
To depend
Solely on words.

But then the words wouldn't come
And there was silence again
It sank in like stones in water
And melted into the familiarity of
blank stares.

Piece by piece, it began to undo
The sound that was uniquely theirs.

THE STREET

The street bleeds
                    Salty tears
                    Salty beer
Spilled from either too little love
Or too much of a good thing
And it waits for
                    Feet that ache
                    Feet that dance
To lumber along
Or step to distant rhythms

The street knows secrets
                    Collects joy
                    Collects pain

As it silently waits
For the rain to wash its slate
clean

A HEART HOLDS MANY SECRETS

*You captured the moon in your
arms
And I fell by the wayside
No light is there for me
Here in this place of darkness
I dwell among shadows
Frightened of the light
And what it will reveal
I am comfortable hiding
This secret place is mine alone
Out of sight and writing down
verses
My heart is unreachable
For it belongs to one
Whose arms are already full*

PRECIOUS MOMENTS

I awake to the sound of rain

Your arms envelope me

Your tender whispers

Beg me to remain

As I snuggle against

Your warmth

The ceiling fan whirs above us

Curtains billow

Pictures on the dresser

Stare in wonder

Jealous of what they see

The clock keeps ticking

Though I beg for it to stop

I don't want to go!

These moments are too precious,

Too few

Still, forever they will linger

HOPE IN THE RAIN

*Cold fingers trace circular
raindrops on the window*

*Mosaics of umbrellas line the
street*

Mist dances on the rooftop

*While soft music gently sweeps
across the porch*

And tired,

Hungry

Feelings

Go to sleep

Keeping hope alive

Amongst the rain ...

Robert A. Cozzi

THE SOUND OF YOUR VOICE

The silence is poking at my ear
A cloudburst of thoughts brings me
here
Giving shapes to the feelings
That each of my rain drenched
thoughts evoke

Beyond belief
I crave the sound of your voice
To give me reprieve
From this quiet inferno

Colorful words like
Love, hope, faith and desire
Flow easily from my pen…bringing
back your audible presence
And eclipsing the unnerving silence

Your silence penetrates my core
But even if I scream
At the top of my lungs
Your silence will just drown me out

THE SOUND OF WATER FALLING

I lost myself tonight
Under a steady waterfall
Of dreams
And in the arms
Of new-fangled love

Love's fire and flames
Surrounded me with warmth
And your smile
Twinkled in my eyes

It was finally our time
To just be
What fate intended for us all
along...

SUMMER SHADOWS

All along the bike trail
Our shadows race
Just ahead of us
Toward shade that waits
Where the silver lake bends road
And aquatic flowers
Drink what dribbles
Down the lake's sloped chin

Late afternoon sun
Begins its rest
Across fresh cut grass
As we settle in
Sitting back to back
In silence
Until we can no longer
Keep our heavy eye lids from
closing...

STARING AT CLOUDS
HIGH ABOVE THE BEACH
IN NORTH CAROLINA

Vacant clouds
That have lost their way
Spill sodden secrets
Onto deaf ears
And lonely cups
Fill them with salty water

APOGEE

Our toes squish in the sand
Waves tickle and dance around
our feet
The ocean breeze whips by our
heads

Inside the stillness, a lonely
seagull cries out
While we walk the deserted
shoreline alone
Hand in hand, huddled in our
hooded sweatshirts

Up ahead we spot
Two sand castles

*Beautifully appointed with
shells and sea glass*

*With the arrival of high
tide...we watch
As they slowly wash back out
to sea
Good-bye summer...*

Acknowledgements

I would like to express my thanks to:
Mary Healy Davis, Aileen Mueller, Ian
Tompkins, A.S.Angelo, Phillip Wilcher,
Deborah Cantor-Adams, Tai Babilonia, Jane
Babineau, Jack Babineau, Nancy Darrow,
Karin Tirrell Hoffmann, Nancy Kaiser,
Mary McElhone, Sandra Iammatteo, Garrett
Zavaglia, Steven Kelley, Danielle Hafler-
Porosky, Lorrie Kwasek Antczak, Rebecca
Tartoni, Jason Monterling, Nick Nascelli,
Kristin Nascelli, Nicholas Nascelli, Ruby
Wyer, Monica McDermott, Matthew
Woolfrey, Paul Kocum, Walt Clarkson,
Victor Hoff, Jamie Lamarra, Ellie Sullivan,
Katy Daly, Rob Shipley, John Janner, Brian
Kelly, Stewart Rodgers, Jill Jones, Jaime
Schneider, Diane Marie Carney, Tyler
Slemp, Osvaldo Paese, Shelly Marie Baril,
Phil Baril, Gene Koose, Anthony Keating,
Annette Cozzi, Morgan Ansons, Duncan
Ewart, Ron Haselden, Matthew Mayfield,
Justin Pypniowski, Kimberly Kandel-Basile,
Jeanne Emerick, Suzy Hone, Tom Smart, Jo
Ann Marie Salmoretti, Angela Elsbree,
Trish Biznik Abell, Neal Acito, Frances
Tompkins, Kathleen Braun Cavallo, Donnie
W. Sanders, Hunter Reeve, Ryan Smith,

Haley Neibergall, JC Van Luyn, Michael Protoski. Additionally, The poet Lo, Stevie Nicks, my Facebook and You Tube friends, and to my Mom, Claire Bride Cozzi, for being my writing mentor.

24341932R00045

Made in the USA
Charleston, SC
20 November 2013